Exponential Growth: The Surge Strategies to Take Your Business to New Heights

Introduction

Welcome to an empowering journey that will transform your approach to exponential growth. This comprehensive handbook distills cutting-edge frameworks, digital strategies, and leadership approaches to surge your business to new heights.

Imagine your company expanding at an incredible rate, with your vision unfolding into reality. This book is your roadmap, with growth icon John Bouter as your experienced guide. His proven methodology has enabled stagnant businesses to thrive.

John's profound insights will be your trusted companion. This book dives deep into every aspect of exponential growth – from crafting vision to celebrating milestones. You'll master strategic frameworks, digital transformation, team empowerment, and more. Each chapter provides detailed understanding to orchestrate your company's ascent.

Your journey will teach you the intricacies of strategy, the immense power of digital, and the value of a motivated team. You'll learn how to refine approaches, overcome challenges, and sustain momentum. Most importantly, you'll discover how to embrace agile evolution and lifelong growth.

In conclusion, you'll have the mindset and tools to propel your company into new realms of success. Exponential advancement is within reach through John's guidance and proven techniques.

The path begins by examining stagnation to uncover the route to better growth. Progress starts with comprehension – a foundation this book will provide.

Are you ready to realize your company's possibilities? Then open your mind, buckle up, and prepare to embark on the first step toward exponential success. Your transformative journey starts here.

Chapter 1: Breaking Through Stagnation

Frustrated growth and unmet potential – these phrases encapsulate the dilemma facing countless service businesses. Though investing in marketing, returns often disappoint, causing doubt and frustration. In this chapter, we'll dive deep into the layers of stagnation to uncover the issues inhibiting sustainable growth.

Imagine eagerly awaiting your campaign results only to find lackluster engagement and revenue. As the underwhelming data trickles in, disappointment displaces excitement. What went wrong? Were the strategies flawed? Does an elusive formula for exponential growth exist? This feeling of stalled progress encapsulates the stagnation dilemma.

Meet John Bouter, the founder of Exxecsys Digital and seasoned expert in enabling transformational growth. John has faced stagnation himself and intimately understands the challenges you experience. Through decades of strategic innovation, he has successfully transcended stagnation to unlock exponential growth for organizations across industries. Visualize John as your sage guide through stagnation into uncharted realms of success.

But why does stagnation persist for so many businesses? What systemic issues impede progress and prevent organizations from sustaining exponential growth? The answers reveal an intricate lattice of factors encompassing the ever-evolving landscape of consumer behaviors, accelerating digital advancements, intensifying competition, complacency with mediocrity, and reluctance to take risks. In a world of unprecedented change, traditional linear approaches to growth feel increasingly ineffective for many.

View this chapter as a catalyst to embrace a profoundly transformative perspective on your organization's potential. Envision entirely new realms of achievement beyond what was previously imagined. This chapter illuminates the fact stagnation is not a judgment of your capabilities or commitment. Rather it is a beckoning towards a new exponential path – one of visionary leadership, strategic evolution, and boundless possibility.

Each temporary setback and period of uncertainty further hones expertise, as long as such experiences are reflected upon with a growth mindset. Every hurdle encountered strengthens business resilience and grit. Through the course of this book, absorb the deeply held belief that exponential advancement is not reserved for some elite few, but rather is accessible to organizations and leaders who dare to wholeheartedly commit to the journey. Your company, once constrained by stagnation, possesses untapped power to redefine entire industry landscapes. This chapter marks the first step in comprehending the causes of stagnation, in order to subsequently take targeted exponential action.

The journey to exponential success is ripe with promise, but first preparation is required. Are you ready to fundamentally break through stagnation? Then let us examine the key causes of stagnation, and how you can proactively address them:

Consumer Behavior Evolution

The accelerating pace of evolution in consumer preferences, values, and shopping habits is a core contributor to stagnation. Many growth strategies fail to sufficiently account for increasingly dynamic behavior shifts across generational cohorts, as well as within demographics. Without constantly tracking changes and adapting accordingly, strategies will inevitably misalign over time with emerging consumer needs and values.

Signposts that consumer behavior evolution may be a factor in stagnation include flattening sales and engagement metrics, especially with historically reliable customer groups. Plateauing feedback scores, social mentions, or brand sentiment can also signal a consumer behavior misalignment. To address this, businesses must commit to implementing advanced tracking of behavior change, deriving insights through analysis, and then iteratively aligning strategies and messaging. Agility in product and brand positioning will enable resonance with evolving consumers.

Digital Disruption

The exponential advances in digital technology represent both massive opportunity but also potential disruption if adoption is too slow. Most notably, the social-mobile revolution has radically reshaped B2C interaction and purchasing habits. Yet many businesses still overly focus on traditional channels and lack integrated omni-channel strategies. Without embracing the full spectrum of digital, growth is left on the table.

Signs of stagnation due to lagging digital adoption include declining website traffic and engagement as audiences shift to new platforms. Businesses trapped in analog channels will suffer from lack of data insights that fuel modern decision-making. Siloed processes and fragmented systems also limit an organization's digital agility and velocity. To harness digital disruption for growth, businesses must prioritize integrated mobile and social strategies, implement analytics, and leverage automation.

Intensifying Competition

In many sectors, intensifying competition driven by new innovations and shifting consumer values has reached unprecedented levels. Unless businesses rethink their differentiation and core value proposition, they risk commoditization or displacement. Legacy strengths must be re-evaluated.

Indicators of stagnation due to fiercer competition include declining market share, compressing margins, and loss of talent to hungry competitors. Complacency and lack of competitive insight magnify this risk. To adapt, businesses should re-identify sources of competitive advantage, focus on their core differentiators, and recognize competitors as instructors for how to evolve value propositions.

Culture of Complacency

Cultural complacency, defined as an organizational comfort with modest or mediocre results, dampens the hunger and drive required for exponential growth. Often, a period of linear success will breed problematic satisfaction with minor incremental gains. This limits appetite for further advancement.

Signs of a creeping complacent mindset include lack of urgency, inertia after initial growth spurts, and dwindling strategic prioritization of exponential initiatives. Settling for "good enough" permeates all levels. To reignite exponential aspiration, a culture of resilience, innovation and change must be instilled, along with embedding rituals to constantly challenge yourself. Bring in external perspectives to shake up group-think.

Fear of Risk Taking

An aversion to taking calculated risks out of fear of failure or uncertainty also restricts many organizations. Exponential growth initiatives by nature contain risk, requiring confidence in strategic bets that disrupt the status quo. Avoiding perceived risk causes reliance on outdated but comfortable models.

Indicators of stagnation caused by risk reluctance include defaulting to incremental tweaks over bold innovation. Leadership over-analyzes without pulling the trigger on initiatives with promising but uncertain outcomes. Data paralysis sets in. To counter, bold experiments with impact metrics must be designed, and leadership must accept occasional failure, if key learnings result, as part of the exponential growth journey.

Lack of External Ecosystem Awareness

Finally, stagnation often emerges when businesses do not commit to constantly learning about and tracking developments in the external business ecosystem. This includes market trends, emerging technologies, competitor innovations, and shifts in public sentiment. Insularity causes blind spots.

When leadership excessively focuses inwards vs. gathering external intelligence, strategies lag behind changes until it's too late. Reversing this requires dedicating resources to gathering ecosystem insights through research, expert counsel, data analysis and building diverse networks, then collaboratively applying those learnings.

In summation, stagnation is multifaceted, but diagnosable and addressable through awareness, accountability and strategic adjustment. Exponential growth requires first comprehending why traditional linear approaches fail to sustain meaningful progress. Then leaders can make the mindset shifts and capability investments needed to power growth well beyond incremental gains.

Change brings opportunity but also demands risk, courage and work. With the right vision and perspective, stagnation can transform into unstoppable momentum. This chapter provides the foundation to commence that journey. Now, let us explore the strategies to ignite growth. Starting with adopting an exponential vs. linear mindset – the prerequisite to unlocking your organization's boundless potential. Onward!

Chapter 2: Developing an Exponential Mindset

Linear growth and incremental progress will only take organizations so far in today's exponentially changing world. To ignite truly transformational growth, leaders must shift mindsets from linear to exponential – embracing bold new frameworks for realizing tenX or 100X goals over 10X. This chapter provides the roadmap for developing an exponential mindset, providing the mental foundation to then architect and lead exponential initiatives.

Imagine an expansive circle, symbolizing exponential growth, contrasted with a straight line showing linear progression. Your organization likely exists somewhere on that linear path today. Now envision industry leaders 20 steps ahead on an exponential trajectory, almost disappearing over the horizon. John Bouter, having led his own exponential journey, understands this mindset shift intimately. He will be your sherpa guide on this mental journey into the foothills of exponential thinking.

What differentiates an exponential vs. linear mindset? First, exponential leaders operate from an abundance mentality seeing endless opportunity, while linear is constrained by assumptions of limitations. Exponential pursues step function leaps, while linear seeks incremental gains. Exponential leaders believe 10X goals, while linear settles for 10% growth aims. Ultimately, exponential fundamentally re-imagines possibility, while linear works within existing paradigms.

This chapter will map the key shifts required to embrace exponential over linear thinking. As you read each section, picture your mind opening to a vast new landscape of potential and opportunity for your organization. Expanding your mental horizons is the critical first step to then guiding your company to exponential heights. With an exponential mindset, no achievement lies beyond reach.

Cultivate an Abundance Mentality

The exponential leader sees abundance and opportunity where others see scarcity and limits. External constraints are reconstructed as expansive possibilities when viewed through an exponential lens. Competitors become partners. Challenges become lessons. Roadblocks become springboards. This abundance mentality liberates exponential leaders from mental boxes and limitations, opening vistas of tenX possibilities.

Start by reframing any limiting beliefs about your organization or market. Then expand your aperture three hundred and sixty degrees to scan the environment for partnership possibilities. Finally, catalog challenges you face and reframe them through an exponential opportunity lens. These exercises will widen your mental aperture and unearth hidden pathways.

Believe in the Impossible

"Impossible is not a fact, but an opinion" stated entrepreneur Peter Diamandis. Exponential leaders live this, internally holding the belief that 10X goals are not fantasies but achievable objectives given the right strategy and commitment. Grounded optimism, passion, and an internal locus of control allow exponentials to envision the "impossible", then work tirelessly to make it reality.

Catalog the "impossible" goals for your organization, the ones that feel just out of reach. Write them in the present tense as if currently true to crystallize them in your mind. Then chart a provisional pathway to these goals by imagining you have unlimited resources. Finally, identify the first three steps you can take right now to get this goal sequence started. These belief exercises breathe life into exponential goals.

Adopt a Creator vs. Victim Mentality

Exponential leaders view themselves not as passive victims of external forces, but active creators of new realities. This instills confidence and momentum during difficult times. Creators see opportunities everywhere, while victims see obstacles. Creators control their mindsets, while victims let environments control them. By focusing energy on creating vs. resisting, exponentials shape rather than react to circumstances.

When encountering roadblocks, ask yourself "how can I create a solution?" to spark new pathways. Celebrate small daily progress to reinforce your creator identity. And find ways to shape your environment through leadership, initiative and positive influence. Cumulatively, these habits instill a creator mentality that enables exponential achievement.

Develop a 10X Vision

Exponential leaders architect 10X visions that redefine what is perceived as possible. Rather than extrapolating the present, they envision a future radically different on every dimension. 10X visions are emotionally inspirational, creating a massive force that pulls companies forward. Audacious visions also liberate imagination and innovation, driving exponential progress.

Using the abundance, belief, and creator mindsets, draft a 10X vision for your company or team. Make it boldly aspirational. Ensure it taps intrinsic motivations. Paint a vivid portrait of a transformed future. And infuse it with optimism and conviction. This will unleash your exponential vision which then becomes the north star guiding your journey.

Make Little Bets

Exponentials avoid monolithic projects with binary outcomes. Instead they run many small experiments through "little bets" - modest investments testing new ideas to glean learning and build conviction behind bigger moves. Little bets not only maximize learning, they compound momentum through small wins that accelerate capability. Losses become inexpensive instruction.

Rather than extensive planning, start executing small experiments to test concepts. Ensure they are time-boxed and low cost. Leverage tools like MVPs and prototyping to accelerate learning cycles. Celebrate both wins and failures for their invaluable instruction. Make this testing and iteration muscle a core competence. Cumulatively, little bets enable big exponential leaps.

Embrace Failure

Exponential leaders do not just tolerate failure, they extract its strategic value. Failed experiments provide priceless learning, while the resilience gained by pushing through failure compounds exponential capabilities. Thomas Edison famously said of his experiments "I have not failed. I've just found 10,000 ways that won't work". Exponentials embrace this mindset.

Catalog recent failures or setbacks, both big and small. Identify the key lessons learned from each experience. Consider crafting an organizational "failure hall of fame" to reinforce learning from disappointments. And remember that each fall presents an invaluable opportunity to develop grit and resilience that will enable later exponential success. Extract all learning value from failure.

Take Intelligent Risks

Exponential initiatives necessitate taking calculated risks to break from the status quo. Exponential leaders are not reckless gamblers. But they are willing to make strategic bets on promising but uncertain innovations ahead of perfect information. Intelligent risks boldly seize opportunity while also rapidly incorporating learnings to course correct.

Assess key risks blocking your bolder initiatives and vision. Outline strategies for mitigating major downsides even for worst case scenarios. Then stress test your risk analysis through contrarian red teaming. Finally, consider which risks are necessary to progressively desensitize the organization and build risk intelligence. With support, most come to see intelligent risk-taking as fuel for exponential growth vs. instability.

In summary, exponential thinking requires major mental shifts from conventional linear mindsets. But making this investment is utterly foundational to then leading exponential achievement. Mastering these mindsets, behaviors and skills will unlock what currently seems just out of reach. This work is challenging but profoundly empowering. And the destination – exponential growth – makes the effort more than worthwhile. It's time to start your exponential journey!

Chapter 3: Crafting an Exponential Vision

Exponential organizations are guided by a bold exponential vision – a vivid portrait of a future 10X or 100X better on critical dimensions than the present. This chapter provides a blueprint for crafting a vision with the inspiration and specificity to ignite exponential growth. Imagine your organization is a rocket ship, and this vision is the guiding star that illuminates the path for your voyage to exponential heights.

Legendary exponential strategist John Bouter has led the creation of exponential visions that disrupted industries. He understands that an exponential vision must be emotionally compelling and strategically galvanizing in order to catalyze action. As you read this chapter, envision John advising you on architecting a vision capable of 10X impact for your organization.

What are the key elements of an exponential vision? First, it is unambiguously exponential, using vivid language depicting a future exponentially better. Second, it taps core human motivations to inspire viral passion. Third, it provides strategic direction by focusing resources on a common goal. The result is a vision that accelerates momentum through clarity, inspiration and alignment.

This chapter provides the blueprint to craft your exponential vision. Each section explains key considerations and techniques. You will emerge more confident in your vision's ability to ignite energy and enable exponential growth. With an exponential vision, you can lead others on the adventure of a lifetime. Let us commence designing a north star guiding your organization's moonshot.

Specify the Exponential Outcomes

Exponential visions must depict a future radically better than today by specific multiples such as 10X or 100X. This quantification sets an exponential stake in the ground that pulls teams forward. Both the exponential target and timeline create clarity on the scale of ambition.

For your key organizational outcomes, define an exponential target and by when - for example growing revenue 100 fold in 5 years. Ensure your aim meets Peter Diamandis' SMART criteria: Specific, Measurable, Attainable, Relevant and Timebound. This exponential goal specificity will drive strategy prioritization and focus efforts for maximum impact.

Make the Vision Emotionally Compelling

Visions must stir passion, excitement and conviction in order to fully motivate. Exponential visions tap into core human motivations such as freedom, growth, justice and legacy. Effective framing includes portraying a positive future state, shared prosperity, and member empowerment. Metaphors, imagery and storytelling techniques further boost engagement.

Catalog the core motivations of your members and stakeholders. Craft vision content and messaging that powerfully resonates with these intrinsic motivations. Share the vision through compelling storytelling, tying it to shared values and aspirations. Use vivid, visual language. Set the vision to inspirational music and cadence. This emotional amplification will ignite exponential energy.

Convey Core Values and Purpose

Visions that powerfully convey core values and purpose trigger deeper passion and commitment from members. Ensure your vision directly expresses the values that form your organizational identity. Bring your purpose to life by describing the better future state you will create. This fosters personal identification with the exponential vision.

Clearly list your organization's core values. Assess how well they currently manifest in culture and strategy. Identify any misalignments. Then integrate the core values centrally within the vision messaging in authentic ways. Clearly articulate your purpose and how achieving this vision will further that purpose. This alignment and transparency will deepen engagement.

Make the Benefits Explicit

Clearly convey the benefits - both qualitative and quantitative - that members and stakeholders will gain from achievement of this vision. Benefits may include financial gains, capability development, status, belonging, purpose fulfillment and more. This reinforces the value proposition of contributing to the exponential vision.

Catalog all major benefits categories relevant to your members and stakeholders. Consider Maslow's hierarchy of needs as well as intrinsic and extrinsic motivation models. Then ensure the vision messaging repeatedly ties into each major benefit category. This reinforcement will amplify motivation and engagement with the exponential vision.

Inject Optimism and Conviction

Optimism and shared conviction are contagious energies that accelerate visions. Demonstrate deep, authentic confidence that this future can be achieved through collective effort. Share inspiring examples of progress. Outline the path ahead.

Boldly state the vision as already unfolding. Such messaging sustains commitment during difficult times.

Identify any countervailing pessimistic tendencies in your culture. Then craft vision messaging to specifically counterbalance with optimism and possibility. Share evidence of early traction. Have leadership repeatedly express unwavering conviction. These injections of optimism lift up the vision and fuel exponential momentum.

Make the Vision Manifest

Exponential visions must transcend words and be made physically manifest through symbols, artifacts and experiences. This brings the vision into tangible reality, making it more accessible and memorable for stakeholders. Manifestations also reinforce consistency of messaging across mediums.

Brainstorm creative ways to make the vision tangible using visual symbols, artwork, physical artifacts, rituals, work spaces, rewards and more. Look for opportunities to create immersive vision experiences. The goal is for members to continually encounter the vision manifested in ways large and small, sustaining engagement.

Refresh and Repurpose the Vision

Though directionally consistent, exponential visions should periodically refresh through tailored delivery for different audiences and contexts. Repurposing using different framing, examples and emphasis sustains engagement over time. Refreshing also allows integration of learnings and environmental changes.

Analyze your various stakeholder groups and settings. Craft tailored messaging that hits key points for each audience while staying directionally aligned. Update vision narratives and examples to integrate latest learnings. Continually emphasize different parts of the vision as needed strategically. Keep the vision vibrant and relevant.

Exponential visions require boldness, heart and constant reinforcement. But with the right vision craftsmanship, you can ignite belief in an extraordinary future for your organization. When powered by a compelling exponential vision, anything is possible. Craft yours today!

Chapter 4: Building an Exponential Plan

Bringing an exponential vision into reality requires an exponential plan - a strategic roadmap guiding teams to achieve 10X objectives over anticipatable horizons. This chapter reveals how to construct an exponential plan that aligns and accelerates resources towards breakthrough ambitions. Envision this plan as the navigational chart for your exponential voyage.

Exponential plans comprise interconnected objectives, key results, and actions forming a lattice of accountability. They also outline exponential technologies and models that act as force multipliers. And they prepare for challenges through contingency planning. With John Bouter's guidance, you will learn to architect exponential plans propelling your team to unprecedented growth.

Let us explore the key elements that comprise an effective exponential plan. Each builds on the others into a cohesive scaffolding. You will emerge ready to craft an exponential plan tailored to your organization's specific context and goals. With a robust exponential plan, your bold vision moves decisively from dreams into reality. Onward to shaping the strategy for your exponential ascent!

Set Massive Yet Feasible Goals

Exponential plans set goals requiring 10-100X outcomes within set timeframes to concentrate efforts. The goal targets should feel daunting yet feasible given total focus. Goals are constructed to create urgency while allowing flexibility on tactics. Less ambitious goals limit results, while unrealistic ones deflate efforts.

Analyze your vision to identify 2-3 goals requiring 10-100X outcomes over coming years. Set ambitious but credible timeframes. Use techniques like backcasting. Stress test draft goals through critique. Set supporting milestones demonstrating progress. Refine until the goals feel just out of reach but achievable with dedication.

Define Key Results

For each exponential goal, define 2-5 objective key results quantifying achievement. Effective key results are specific, measurable, achievable, relevant and timebound. They break goals into manageable yet ambitious milestones marking progress. Tracking key results maintains clear sight on the destination amid day-to-day activities.

For each draft exponential goal, identify component parts that can be made into focused key results. Iteratively refine into SMART criteria. Ensure they ladder up into the overarching goal. Identify leading and lagging indicators to track. Maintain a key result roadmap showing status towards the exponential goals.

Assign Accountability

Each key result must have a directly accountable owner responsible for driving completion. This focuses accountability and priority. Accountability is assigned to roles not individuals to allow flexibility. Exponential plans create a lattice of accountability connecting and coordinating efforts across the organization.

Catalog all key results and identify the single most responsible role for each. Avoid diffusion across multiple unclear owners. Have senior members meet with owners to reinforce accountability and convey authority over resources needed. Maintain an accountability matrix visible across the organization showing owners. Actively manage changes.

Outline Critical Actions

For every key result, detail the 2-3 most critical actions required for completion. This moves the exponential plan from vague vision to concrete execution. Actions should be specific, measurable and time bound. Adapt actions based on new learnings. Maintain a living catalog of current critical actions to guide day-to-day efforts.

Have owners brainstorm critical actions for each of their key results. Refine into clear, discrete activities. Prioritize using importance and urgency criteria. Capture metadata needed for tracking. Maintain a living action register of current priorities reviewed systematically at team meetings. Update status tracking regularly.

Prepare Contingencies

Exponential plans must also anticipate potential barriers and outline contingency options if challenges emerge. This allows rapid adaptation if circumstances change while maintaining forward momentum. Contingency planning also mitigates perceived risk of the exponential plan.

Methodically identify the major contingencies that could derail key results, both internal and external. Outline plausible responses and triggers for rapid deployment as needed. Run contingency exercises to stress test readiness. Maintain an evolving contingency section within the exponential plan. Revisit contingencies proactively as new risks emerge.

Map Exponential Models

Exponential plans specify the exponential technologies and models that will act as force multipliers, such as AI, crowdsourcing, platforms, or leveraging communities. These models dramatically expand capacity, speed, quality and access to resources.

Catalog exponential technologies relevant to your industry and goals. Assess readiness for adoption and implementation paths. Systematically identify where applying exponential models can accelerate key results. Maintain an inventory of exponential force multipliers linked to your plan. Aggressively incorporate models producing asymmetric impact.

Install Rapid Iteration

Rapid iteration sustains progress and learnings from an exponential plan. Continuously updated trackers, regular sync meetings, post-action reviews, and real-time dashboards maintain visibility. Near instant feedback channels allow constant adaptation. Iteration prevents inertia.

Implement agile tracking of all goals, key results, actions and contingencies. Build regular sync rhythms and streamlined decision paths to accelerate iteration. Automate status dashboards for transparency. Develop feedback channels for rapidly surfacing lessons. Empower teams to iterate aggressively. Maintain extreme focus on speed of learning and adaptation.

The above elements integrate into a comprehensive exponential strategic plan. With this living roadmap guiding coordinated execution, your team can ascend to 10X achievements. Tempering bold vision with strategic rigor, an exponential plan turns dreams into reality. Let's build yours now!

Chapter 5: Leading Exponential Teams

Realizing an exponential vision requires building an exponential team - one aligned in purpose, equipped with exponential skill sets, and empowered to take ownership. This chapter reveals how leaders can craft high velocity exponential teams capable of 10X productivity and impact. Picture an exponential rocket, fueled by this empowered team united by mission.

Legendary exponential leader John Bouter understands deeply how to build teams with the mindsets, behaviors and skills to drive exponential outcomes. Throughout his career, John has led exponential transformations by cultivating such groups unified by a sense of exponential purpose. Through his insights, you will learn how to build an exponential team marking your own organization's success story.

Let us explore key strategies for developing exponential teams. Each dimension builds on the others into a cohesive system lifting teams to new heights of performance and fulfillment. You will leave ready to foster an exponential team culture becoming the wind beneath the wings of your organization's exponential ascent.

Instill a Sense of Shared Mission

Exponential teams are ignited by a shared sense of the purpose and urgency of their exponential mission. They view their goal as massively transformative and require each member's contribution to achieve. When infused with mission, teams gain cohesion, motivation and moral authority.

Research shows organizational purpose dramatically multiplies team velocity and satisfaction. Clearly and continuously articulate the exponential mission in ways that resonate at individual levels. Share exponential success stories from the frontlines. Reinforce how each member builds towards the greater vision. Celebrate incremental progress.

Recruit Exponential Talent

Exponential teams require team members equipped with emotional intelligence, learning agility, grit, flow mindsets and solutioning skills enabling nimble navigation of uncertainty. Selection and development is key.

Define in detail the exponential competencies and traits needed. Adapt recruiting approaches to attract exponential talent. Ask exponential interview questions. Do trial projects. Restructure roles and rewards to provide developmental stretch assignments meeting exponential needs. Seed teams with strong exponential role models.

Target 10x Training

Training develops the critical skills that empower exponential team velocity, excellence and flexibility. Targeted exponential training builds strategic muscles and an empowering mindset. Immersive simulations and live scenarios create experiential learning.

Analyze the skills vital for your exponential objectives but currently lacking – insights that training can address. Identify specialized exponential curricula beyond traditional offerings – for example design thinking and lean startup methodologies. Architect immersive learning experiences. Bring in exponential experts for real-time coaching. Maintain a learning lab for continual skills development.

Structure for Speed

Exponential teams operate with agile rhythms, streamlined decision rights and dynamic re-allocation of resources to seize fleeting opportunities. Fluidity of structure breeds responsiveness, intelligence flow and adapting to meet exponential challenges.

Analyze all processes and systems for opportunities to promote increased agility and speed. Flatten information access and visibility. Push decision rights to the edges. Eliminate friction through digitization. Evolve team rhythms to fit exponential goals. Maintain open architectures allowing flexible reconfiguration. Empower teams to morph as needed.

Open Information Flows

Exponential organizations thrive on open information flows and transparency enabling sensing of threats and opportunities in real-time. Exponential teams thus circulate information with radical freedom and openness to power rapid adaptation.

Promote real-time sharing of market intelligence, project learnings and metrics longitudinally across teams. Leverage digital tools to create exponential information flows. Flatten access and remove bottlenecks. Crowdsource insights from the full organization. Dismantle silos slowing information diffusion. Build habits of openness and sharing. Radical transparency allows exponential maneuvering.

Use Exponential Technologies

Exponential teams tap exponential technologies to multiply team productivity, insight and innovation. AI, mobility, automation, platforms and crowdsourcing expand capacity, coordination, sensemaking and creativity.

Catalog relevant exponential technologies each team could productively leverage. Prioritize implementations balancing effort and exponential impact. Transition select tasks to AI and robotic automation to boost capacity. Build collaboration platforms and digital systems to enhance transparency and mobility. Provide state of the art digital capabilities. Set aggressive adoption targets.

Empower Team Autonomy

Exponential organizations push decision authority and task freedom to frontline teams empowered with agency to determine how best to achieve key results. Distributed authority breeds engagement and rapid adaptation by teams closest to the issues.

Audit decision rights and identify opportunities to reassign authority closer to frontlines and information. Define team goals but not rigid methods. Build leadership capability for coaching vs. command & control. Allow teams to configure roles and rhythms fitting goals. Grant reasonable financial autonomy. Guide cultural change towards responsibility and trust. Empower teams with agency.

Celebrate Exponential Wins

Positive reinforcement accelerates exponential behaviors and team velocity through motivation, energy and expanded perceived opportunity. Milestone celebrations refuel teams for the road ahead. Highlight heroes illustrating exponential values.

Praise exponential values and accomplishments at team gatherings. Find opportunities to publicly recognize exponential performance. Schedule special exponential events and milestone celebrations. Award prizes for major exponential contributions. Circulate exponential success stories. Make the positive momentum visible. Celebrate exponential steps forward.

By cultivating empowered exponential teams, leaders can compound momentum towards exponential goals. With dedication, you can build the team taking your organization's future to new heights. Let's get started today!

Chapter 6: Creating Exponential Innovations

Delivering 10X new innovations is a central driver of exponential growth. This chapter reveals how to systematically discover, test and scale disruptive innovations through an exponential innovation engine. Envision this engine fueled by the inspiration, know-how, and tools you will gain from exponential innovation master John Bouter.

John's career has bridged exponential innovation in several industries, leveraging approaches like lean startup, design thinking and agile product development to repeatedly create disruptive innovations and then rapidly commercialize them through exponential scaling. This chapter will allow you to tap into John's framework so your own organization can generate transformative innovations.

Let's begin the journey into building your exponential innovation engine. Each section overviews an innovation gear to design. Together these gears will power your organization's rapid prototyping, experimentation and breakthrough innovations that disrupt complacency. Turning this engine will open up new worlds of possibility. Let's start crafting your exponential innovation machine!

Build a Diverse Innovation Team

Exponential innovation benefits immensely from diverse viewpoints of team members combining different disciplines, backgrounds, demographics and thinking styles. This ecosystem of perspectives unlocks creativity and uncovers insights inaccessible to homogeneous teams.

Analyze your current innovation team composition. Identify missing elements that would add exponentially diverse thinking styles and perspectives. Recruit innovators who demonstrate curiosity, creativity and comfort with uncertainty. Provide collaboration skills to harness the benefits of diversity. Forge an empowered innovation collective open to radical concepts.

Scan the Innovation Horizon

Exponential innovators stay constantly attuned to trends, science and ecosystem shifts scanning for sparks hinting at promising innovation horizons. Scanning builds intuition, pattern recognition and conviction needed to place strategic bets.

Catalog innovation information channels and filters for priority sources. Schedule horizon scanning time for innovators. Develop processes to capture and share sparks. Look across seemingly unrelated domains for transferable insights. Maintain a digital inspiration vault. Regularly communicate horizon scanning insights to surface opportunities. Scan relentlessly.

Leverage Existing Assets

Exponential innovators fully utilize existing assets - IP, data, platforms, partnerships, systems - to create springboards into adjacent markets and opportunities. This capitalization achieves more with less new investment, concentrating resources.

Catalog all underleveraged assets and capabilities. Assess potential applications in other products, markets and business models. Pick 2-3 assets with promising adjacencies. Brainstorm concepts and minimum viable prototypes. Test.

Refine. Scale. Deliberately reapply assets across the broadest opportunity space.

Launch Many Experiments

Exponential innovators launch an overflowing portfolio of ongoing experiments, embracing failure as learning. This fail fast approach rapidly surfaces winning innovations through disciplined trial and error. Much innovation emerges from compounded experience and evolution vs. singular eureka moments.

Define innovation hypotheses and frame them as experiments. Outline falsifiable tests for each using small, rapid prototypes. Leverage lean and agile methods to accelerate experimentation. Conduct 10X the number of innovation trials as typical for your industry. Celebrate learning from both positive and negative results. Accumulate the innovation wisdom emerging from your experiments.

Integrate Exponential Technologies

Infusing innovations with exponential technologies such AI, genomics, robotics or 3D printing can multiply impact 10X. Layering these exponentials onto concepts creates watershed innovations primed for exponential growth.

Deeply research exponentials with relevance for your market. Assess applications to current and prospective innovations. Envision concepts combining exponentials with products, services or business models. Build experimental prototypes at low cost and risk. Pursue a portfolio of experiments across exponentials. Be aggressive in tapping accelerating exponential technologies.

Rapidly Prototype Promising Concepts

Moving promising concepts quickly from low fidelity prototypes into higher resolution MVPs generates validated learnings while concentrating resources only on successful trajectories. Distributed rapid prototyping scales innovation.

Standardize an agile prototyping development and review process. Equip innovators with common tools and templates. Set guidelines encouraging crude but fast initial prototyping. Implement lightweight digital review methods. Progress only successful concepts to higher fidelity. Prototype early, prototype often, prototype everywhere.

Test Disruptive Business Models

Truly exponential innovations leverage disruptive business models spanning platforms, marketplaces, subscription services, lateral pricing or freemium. Exponential economics surpasses linear gains. Test alternate models.

Analyze traditional economics in your industry for disruption opportunities. Research new business models and examples from other sectors. Envision disruptive models applied to your concepts. Develop lightweight business case prototypes and metrics. Launch market tests of model variants. Be prepared to disrupt existing models with new exponential economics.

Accelerate Time to Market

Fast execution getting innovations to market ahead of competition is critical. Exponential innovators build capabilities reducing time to market 10X via agile development, customer co-creation and modular architectures.

Analyze current product development workflows for bottlenecks and cycle time reduction opportunities through digitization, automation and parallel workflows. Compress release MVP scope through customer focus groups. Pursue open and modular designs allowing faster enhancement. Set stretch goals of 10X reductions in time to market. Maintain maniacal focus on accelerating velocity and release cadences.

Scale Exponentially

Finally, commercializing innovations for exponential growth requires identifying and resourcing scalable adoption channels, pursuing viral marketing, leveraging market platforms and networks, and amplifying through innovation ecosystems. Scalable exponential diffusion is planned from the outset.

Research scalable diffusion models in your industry and analogous ones. Identify potential exponential adoption channels. Envision viral marketing hacks built into product design. Plan leveraging scalable infrastructures like platforms, marketplaces and partner ecosystems for cross promotion. Install rapid iteration to accelerate system optimization. Architect innovations for exponential uptake from the ground up.

With a high velocity exponential innovation engine, organizations can repeatedly create, test and scale 10X innovations disrupting complacency. Combining strategy, diversity, technology and speed, the exponential innovation regime revolutionizes R&D economics. Exponential innovation unlocks tomorrow's possibilities today. It's time to build your engine!

Chapter 7: Developing Exponential Networks

Tapping the power of external ecosystems multiplies exponential impact through leveraged resources, shared infrastructure, and new synergies. This chapter reveals how to design and orchestrate vibrant exponential innovation networks accelerating growth. Envision exponential networks as central nervous systems transmitting signals and energies to all members.

Over his leadership journey, John Bouter has architected exponential networks boosting innovation and growth across organizations. He understands the protocols and architectures enabling networks to self-organize around bold visions. This chapter will provide you the tools to ignite an exponential network that becomes an unstoppable force propelling your organization forward.

Let us explore key strategies for developing exponential networks. Combined, these design elements create living, responsive exponential networks facilitating flow, inspiration, trust and collective achievement. With an exponential network, no organization needs to walk alone on the exponential journey. Now let's begin plotting an exponential network elevating your entire ecosystem.

Promote a Shared Exponential Purpose

Exponential networks form around a shared purpose such as a Big Hairy Audacious Goal requiring collaboration to achieve. This superordinate goal provides the keystone allowing network alignment and coordinated action even across competitors.

Facilitate dialogue to define a shared exponential purpose for potential network members. Frame the exponential destination as only achievable through cooperation. Highlight each player's contribution. Continuously evangelize and embed this exponential purpose across the ecosystem. Let the exponential mission attract members.

Design a Collaborative Architecture

Effective exponential networks design interaction architectures, rhythms, and coordination mechanisms enabling open yet organized collaboration across the full network. Architecture reduces friction and accelerates shared workstreams.

Outline optimal cross-network team structures and rhythms facilitating collaboration towards the shared exponential goal.

Design digital systems enabling transparency, dialogue, and knowledge sharing. Appoint community facilitators to coordinate activities. Evolve architecture iteratively based on member feedback to increase value. Match form to function.

Foster Diversity of Perspectives

Exponential networks intentionally cultivate diversity of thought, backgrounds, disciplines and demographics to harness collective intelligence, boost innovation, and unlock exponential thinking. Diversity empowers the ecosystem.

Audit network diversity across multiple dimensions – organizations, industries, geographies, cultures, professions. Actively develop strategies to fill network diversity gaps and attract missing perspectives. Promote appreciative inquiry and integrative thinking. Provide collaboration skills training. Learn to leverage member differences as keys to shared innovation strength.

Transfer Exponential Skills

Exponential networks accelerate capability development across all members through active coaching, training programs, and skills transfer. Rising tides of exponential skills lift all boats.

Conduct an exponential skills gap analysis for members. Develop targeted exponential trainings and workshops. Incentivize coaching and carve out time for it. Showcase best demonstrated exponential practices for replication. Leverage shared knowledge repositories. Transferring exponential skills liberates collective potential.

Cultivate a Trust Ethos

Exponential networks flourish through deeply cultivated trust enabling open collaboration, radical transparency, shared risk taking, and honest relationships among members. Trust unlocks exponential potential.

Encourage informal social interactions to build familiarity. Use workshops to forge shared purpose and values. Practice assuming positive intent. Adopt protocols protecting confidential information. Demonstrate trust consistently through actions. Promote a secure membership identity and brand. Work ceaselessly towards establishing trust with members.

Apply Exponential Technologies

Exponential networks tap exponential technologies to multiply collaboration velocity, transparency, insight harvesting and innovation. Exponential tech creates network force multipliers.

Research relevant exponential technologies for supercharging networks – AI, AR/VR, predictive analytics, blockchain, crowdsourcing platforms. Evaluate applications against shared goals. Develop implementation roadmaps and move aggressively to integrate exponential technologies enabling members. Tech both powers and is powered by exponential networks.

Coordinate Synchronized Action

While decentralized, exponential networks also require mechanisms to coordinate synchronized collective action on priorities. This balances autonomy with alignment. Lightweight coordination accelerates big collaborations.

Create common calendars and platforms to enhance visibility into member initiatives. Develop proposal processes for members to pitch network-wide campaigns. Convene working groups around priority goals. Use consistent project rhythms and digitized workflows. Provide coordination resources to orchestrate complex multi-party efforts. Synchronization unlocks powerful exponential outcomes.

Celebrate the Network

Exponential networks are strengthened by actively celebrating the collective and promoting a shared identity. Showcasing successes creates positive contagion and engagement. Highlighting the community builds allegiance.

Brand the exponential network to foster a shared identity. Widely publicize collaborations and member contributions. Develop network rituals and ceremonies. Facilitate civil discourse to resolve conflicts. Promote network itself as an enabler of extraordinary innovation and impact for all members. Build a positive exponential community.

By cultivating empowered exponential networks, organizations tap into forces greater than themselves. You can architect an exponential vortex accelerating development, innovation, knowledge and abundance for all members. Exponential networks represent a new form of institutional power in modern economies. It's time to architect one accelerating your organization and entire ecosystem. Let's get started!

Chapter 8: Leveraging Exponential Partnerships

Forming selective exponential partnerships multiplies resources, capabilities, and impact through combined synergies with mutually aligned organizations. This chapter provides the playbook to identify, structure, and cultivate game-changing exponential partnerships driving breakthrough growth.

Over his leadership journey, John Bouter has engineered numerous exponential partnerships that became cornerstones enabling his organizations' exponential ascent. The partnerships allowed John's teams to run faster and reach higher by skillfully leveraging aligned capabilities from the partner entities. This chapter allows you to benefit from John's framework so your own organization can structure exponential partnerships elevating all participating organizations.

Let's examine core strategies for structuring win-win exponential partnerships of lasting value. Each partnership element scaffolds onto the others to create a durable and dynamic platform for exponential growth through joint leverage. Thoughtfully combining these design principles will amplify your partnership outcomes. Now let's begin mapping the path to your exponential partnerships.

Target Exponential Potential

Exponential partnerships require clear identification of the specific exponential goals the partnership will unlock that neither party could efficiently achieve alone. This powers selection of partners with asymmetric potential to meet exponential aims.

Catalog 2-3 exponential goals your organization is pursuing that partnerships could significantly accelerate. Research potential partners with complementary assets and goals to jointly achieve them. Assess partnership scenarios. Analyze projected exponential impact vs alternatives. The most promising opportunities set direction.

Ensure Mission Alignment

Exponential partnerships require collaboration between organizations closely aligned on core values, purpose and exponential vision. Tight mission alignment enables enduring partnerships not blown off course by temporary market shifts or challenges.

Compare potential partner mission statements, values and visions to assess fit. Interview leaders to analyze alignment on exponential goals and culture. Review track records for consistency and community impact. Mission harmony is the foundation for navigating ups and downs together.

Structure for Flexibility

Effective exponential partnerships adopt flexible, agile legal
and operating structures facilitating adaptation as win-win
opportunities emerge over time. Flexibility sustains
exponential partnerships.

Consider broad framework agreements allowing customization
into specific workstream partnerships without extensive
contract renegotiation. Build in mechanisms for periodically
revisiting and updating operating models. Maintain open and
frequent leadership communication channels. Create
lightweight coordination rhythms. Architect for agility.

Appoint Partner Champions

Exponential partnerships are catalyzed by empowered
exponential growth champions within each organization who
take personal responsibility for managing the partnership.
Their conviction sustains partnerships through turbulence.

Identify credible, high initiative internal exponential advocates
to steward the partnership. Ensure they have influence across
their organization but also meaningful autonomy to construct
the collaboration. Support them with resources and executive

air cover. Have partners co-develop an exponential partnership playbook codifying processes. Champions act as the glue.

Co-Create an Exponential Roadmap

Exponential partnerships thrive through jointly authored roadmaps coordinating reciprocal contributions over 3-5 year horizons. Roadmaps align on priorities while allowing customization into detailed action plans.

Schedule an exponential partnership design summit for leaders to draft a multi-year roadmap based on the projected environment. Identify key milestones and workstreams. Define success indicators. Align planning, budget and resource allocation cycles. Annually renew the roadmap while allowing flexibility. Co-direction powers enduring exponential partnerships.

Exchange Exponential Skills

Exponential partnerships multiply capability building by facilitating reciprocal exchange of complementary exponential skills between partners through training, mentorship, people exchange, and sites of practice.

Catalog current exponential skill gaps of each partner. Identify offsetting complementary strengths. Structure exchanges through guest teachers, embedded mentors, staff rotations and team field trips. Share exponential tools and methods. Cross-train using case studies. Knowledge sharing elevates all.

Combine Exponential Assets

Combining mutually beneficial resources, IP, platforms, data, brands, customers and other assets creates partnership force multipliers exceeding standalone efforts. Resource pooling powers synergies.

Map each organization's exponential assets like brands, tech platforms, data reservoirs, patents and global infrastructure. Prioritize highest potential combined applications. Develop licensing, joint R&D and integrated marketing initiatives. The whole exceeds the sum of parts.

Engineer Exponential Innovations

Exponential partnerships unlock exponential innovation through joint R&D projects blending complementary capabilities. Shared risk lowers barriers. Idea cross-pollination sparks creativity.

Define innovation challenges suitable for paired approaches. Assemble joint exponential innovation teams. Provide collaboration tools and frameworks. Accelerate idea flow through cross-organization events and digital channels. Validate concepts through rapid parallel prototyping. Exponential partnerships breed exponential innovations.

The above elements combine into enduring, dynamic exponential partnerships generating abundant exponential value. Exponential partnerships represent a force multiplier applied to your organization's core strategy. Crafted effectively, they can unlock unprecedented growth. It's time to map your exponential partnerships. Onward!

Chapter 9: Installing Exponential Marketing

Exponential marketing approaches engage customers with inspiration versus interruption, deliver 10X more value than expected, and spread contagiously through customer networks to accelerate exponential adoption. This chapter provides the blueprint to engineer viral, customer-centric exponential marketing driving exponential growth.

Over his leadership journey, John Bouter has developed breakthrough exponential marketing campaigns leading customers to new realms of value. John understands how crafting marketing as a generous service earns audience attention and trust, enabling exponential growth vs. treating it as an annoying cost. This chapter will allow you to benefit from John's framework to create marketing that wins hearts and changes minds.

Let's explore the mindsets and methods for engineering marketing that customers love enough to spread. Combined, these exponential marketing keys unlock growth for your organization through service to others. Your marketing will become a gift so meaningful your customers can't help but share it. Now let's begin designing your exponential marketing.

Adopt a Generous Mindset

Exponential marketing starts with genuinely seeking to enrich customers' lives versus treating them as transactions. Marketing designed as a selfless gift builds trust and community enabling exponential growth.

Catalog ways your exponential offerings could help specific customer segments accomplish their life goals and dreams. Identify struggles and friction points marketing could address. Engineer your marketing as a generous gift to guide customers to fulfillment. Check that all marketing efforts pass this generosity test.

Obsess Over Customer Experience

Analyze every micro-moment of your customers' experience across the entire journey to identify opportunities to surprise and delight at exponential levels. Experience drives viral advocacy.

Map your complete end-to-end customer experience. Look for pain points. Envision deliverables 10X better than industry norms. Co-design ideal journeys with clients. Identify opportunities to astound through exponential service and value. Deliver magical customer experiences.

Pursue a Marketing Cadence

Effective exponential marketing follows a drumbeat cadence engaging audiences across multiple touchpoints with consistently compelling content. Sustained cadence breeds familiarity and loyalty.

Define an integrated multi-channel content calendar and release rhythm optimized for your buyer journeys. Pursue consistent brand messaging across channels and campaigns.

Sprinkle surprise and delight moments. Maintain top-of-mind presence through an exponential content drumbeat.

Produce Insightful Content

Produce content delivering truly transforming value by addressing audiences' highest priority needs and goals. Insightful content earns audience attention and achieves exponential marketing returns.

Catalog target audience goals, pain points and defining aspirations. Identify content formats matching audience preferences. Recruit exponential thought leaders to create genuinely transforming content. Repurpose across formats and channels. Promote content through partnerships. Measure engagement and refine. Deliver 10X value through content.

Leverage Influencers

Exponential marketing leverages credible influencers respected by target audiences to accelerate credibility and adoption. Supporter voices drive exponential trust.

Identify key influencers and assess reach with your target segments. Provide exponential user experiences for influencers to share. Craft win-win influencer partnership models respecting their goals. Make it smooth for influencers to advocate on your behalf. Amplify influencer content across your channels. Trusted voices accelerate exponential marketing.

Engineer Viral Loops

Viral loops engineer exponential sharing, network effects and incentives into marketing programs and offerings to drive exponential growth. Virality is designed into the DNA.

Analyze customer journeys for organic viral sharing opportunities. Idea generation workshops can surface possibilities. Add social sharing features in products and campaigns. Structure benefits for referring others and highlight them. Make it frictionless for users to spread your message. Monitor results iteratively and double down on successes. Viral loops enable exponential adoption.

Gather Exponential Insights

Exponential marketing measures holistic impact on customers beyond isolated metrics through journey mapping, NPS and value-based frameworks. True success is measured in enriched lives.

Define a quantified view of total customer value and experience. Survey key journey moments. Calculate incremental lifetime value. Analyze churn drivers. Interview lost customers. The most powerful metrics capture your true exponential impact on lives. Let those guide marketing.

Through these strategies, exponential marketing becomes a mechanism to massively spread value while earning audience attention and advocacy. It becomes a flywheel accelerating your organization's growth through service. By giving more than asked, your marketing gains exponential returns. Get ready for liftoff!

Chapter 10: Installing Exponential Sales

Exponential sales models engage prospective clients with education, deliver 10X value, build community and only then activate revenue opportunities. This chapter reveals how to engineer consultative, value-first sales driving exponential growth through service.

John Bouter has developed several breakthrough exponential sales models generating billions in revenue by putting audience needs first. He understands that by truly helping prospects excel, exponential sales opportunities follow. This chapter allows you to benefit from John's framework for designing consultative sales unlocking exponential growth.

Let's explore the mindsets and methods underpinning consultative sales models. Combined, these keys enable selling through service versus pressure sales. Your sales organization will become advisors clients trust versus vendors hawking wares. Get ready to install exponential sales.

Adopt an Advisor Mindset

Exponential salespeople adopt advisor mindsets seeking to understand client needs and provide genuine solutions. They focus first on value provided before ever discussing revenue. This builds enduring trust.

Catalog common prospect goals and friction points. Analyze how your offerings can guide them to excellence. Craft sales interactions as free consulting addressing client needs before mentioning your solution. Have salespeople take advisor training and shadow trusted counselors. Instill a mission to truly help.

Inform and Educate

Exponential sales models lead with insight - sharing information, perspectives and frameworks allowing prospects to excel. Education builds authority and trust enabling exponential sales relationships.

Identify the knowledge most valuable for your clients' success. Craft engaging education experiences through content, events and tools to provide this. Have experts instruct prospects on excelling before discussing sales. Become known as the informer in your category. Insights attract exponentially more prospects.

Focus on Fit

Exponential sales models patiently invest time validating fit between solutions and prospect needs before driving purchase decisions. Taking time to listen pays exponential dividends long term.

Train salespeople to ask questions focused on deeply understanding prospect goals and contexts. Avoid presenting solutions before proving fit. Have advisors summarize back the client situation. Guide prospects only if a solution truly addresses their needs. Exponential sales align value to needs.

Community Before Commerce

Exponential sales foster community between clients enabling collective learning, support and inspiration. People buy from people. Community builds the relationships that enable exponential sales.

Host events, forums and experiences allowing prospects to interact. Facilitate peer learning and support. Highlight client advocates and success stories. Develop member rituals and traditions. Nurture relationships between prospects first, products second. Community pre-sells for you.

Provide Exponential Value

Exponential sales deliver 10X the insight, impact and transformation buyers expect. Overdelivering earns attention and trust while demonstrating your exponential difference.

Study what overwhelms clients today. Envision values 10X better through exponential innovation. engineer sales interactions providing incredible value before any revenue discussion. Have advisors brainstorm exponential ways to guide client impact. Deliver 10X the transformation clients expect.

Make Buying Effortless

Exponential sales models work relentlessly to remove all friction from the purchase process through radical transparency, automation and simplification. Effortlessness builds lifetime loyalty.

Map your entire sales workflow from prospect to customer identifying pain points. Digitize wherever possible. Reduce steps through automation. Eliminate surprises or complexities. Make pricing transparent and accessible. Guide clients seamlessly from education to delighted customer. Exponential sales are effortless.

Grow Customers Exponentially

Exponential sales support clients' long-term exponential growth through continuity programs, coaching and milestone celebrations expanding usage. Growing clients makes sales continuous.

Define usage milestones by segment and develop supporting materials. Install onboarding, training and coaching programs guiding growth. Highlight and celebrate client exponential successes. Build loyalty programs for continuity purchases. Orchestrate touchpoints guiding clients to new exponential heights.

By elevating sales from transaction Here is more content continuing to service, your organization will earn trust and referrals enabling exponential growth. Leading with value builds relationships that convert and endure. Exponential sales come by seeking first to give. Now go and architect your exponential sales engine!

Chapter 11: Optimizing Exponential Operations

Achieving exponential growth requires reinventing operations to 10X productivity, quality, and flexibility. This chapter reveals how to transform operations into an exponential accelerator through digitization, automation, and empowered teams.

John Bouter has led breakthrough operational transformations across various industries that allowed his organizations to scale exponentially while maintaining quality. John knows that reinventing operations unlocks capacity to meet growing exponential demand. This chapter will provide you with those same exponential operations tools.

Let's examine the key transformations required to overhaul legacy operations into exponential engines. While operations may seem dry, mastering them allows all other exponential initiatives to flourish. With new exponential operations, no demand level will overwhelm your capabilities. Now let's begin installing your exponential operations.

Pursue Hyper Automation

Hyper automation uses robotic process automation, AI, and advanced algorithms to automate routine tasks and processes 10X faster with higher quality and lower costs. This exponential technology revolutionizes productivity.

Analyze all operations workflows and identify automation opportunities through RPA bots, AI systems, and algorithms. Prioritize implementations with highest impact. Develop integration roadmaps. Aggressively expand automation, moving humans into creative roles. Leverage hyper automation to multiply output.

Install Real-Time Dashboards

Exponential operations are guided by real-time data through digital dashboards displaying predictive demand signals, risk indicators, process health metrics and market analytics. Real-time data powers agility.

Define exponential operations metrics across workflows that indicate market changes and process risks. Construct visual dashboards displaying these in real time. Ensure broad data access. Implement monitoring routines and reaction protocols. Real-time exponential operations are data-driven.

Adopt Agile Processes

Agile operations use cross-functional, empowered teams pursuing rapid iteration and continuous improvement to fluidly adapt to changing conditions. Agility enables managing exponential complexity.

Audit processes for agility opportunities through digitization, modularization, outcome orientation and team empowerment. Launch agile pilot teams. Provide agile and collaboration training. Expand successes. Set stretching agile key performance metrics. Agile operations thrive amidst exponential change.

Leverage Ecosystems

Exponential operations tap powerful external partner ecosystems for surge capacity, specialized capabilities, and accelerated innovation. Ecosystem leverage provides flexibility managing exponential volatility.

Catalog external exponential partner capabilities that could ramp production, expertise, and innovation. Prioritize based on impact and build strategic win-win partnerships. Implement tools and platforms to coordinate. Leverage partners for diversity and scale. Ecosystems expand your exponential operations.

Engineer Elastic Scalability

Scalable operations can cost-effectively expand 10X to meet surges in exponential demand through elastic worker pools, modular product architectures and flexible supply chains. This positions organizations to capture exponential opportunities.

Analyze scaling cost structure dynamics and map key parametric dependencies. Prototype and pressure test modular product/service architectures. Develop mixed staffing models balancing elastic and core workers. Build options-based flexible supply chain contracts. Plan to scale while maintaining quality and profitability.

Support Teams Exponentially

Effective exponential operations provide frontline teams exponential support through predictive analytics, digital expert knowledge repos and embedded automation assistants multiplying individual team productivity. Empowered teams enable agility.

Specify productivity barriers for frontline teams. Identify opportunities to provide exponential support through data insights, digitized knowledge, and automated workflows. Pilot AI-enabled assistants. Monitor results and expand successful support models. Support teams to unlock their exponential potential.

Continually Optimize

Optimization sustains exponential operations gains through continually identifying improvement opportunities, running controlled experiments, implementing tested enhancements and refreshing system designs. Optimization instills exponential thinking.

Build hypothesis-driven experimentation into all operations workflows to test improvement ideas. Standardize information flows to share learnings across teams. Dedicate resources to iteration. Maintain a rolling implementation pipeline to operationalize proven optimizations. Continual optimization sustains exponential operations.

The strategies above combine to reinvent operations as a foundation enabling exponential growth versus a bottleneck restraining it. Exponential operations not only power today's surges, but constantly progress to support 10X greater demand tomorrow. Now go unleash your exponential operations!

Chapter 12: Creating Exponential Profit Models

Capitalizing on exponential growth requires reinventing profit models to capture nonlinear economics through subscription models, market platforms, and zero marginal cost models. This chapter provides the strategies to architect profit models that scale exponentially.

John Bouter has repeatedly reinvented profit models across various industries to unlock exponential revenue surges and margin expansion. Traditional linear models leave enormous value on the table. John developed radically innovative profit models that incentivized exponential growth. This chapter will give you those same tools.

Let's examine the key profit model components enabling exponential monetization at scale. Each element builds on the others to create nonlinear profit engines. Thoughtfully combining these concepts will multiply your profitability as demand surges. Now let's begin mapping your exponential profit model.

Leverage Subscription Models

Recurring subscription models based on ongoing access vs. one-time transactions enable exponential revenue scaling by multiplying lifetime customer value through reduced churn and continuous revenue.

Identify opportunities to convert fixed transactions into subscriptions providing continuous differential value. Consult clients to design optimally tiered plans. Develop switch incentives and loyalty programs. Use cohorts to measure revenue expansion and churn. Structure for recurring exponential revenue.

Install Platform Business Models

Platform models connecting distinct groups - buyers & sellers, hosts & renters, drivers & riders - generate exponential network effects as more users attract more users. The platform then monetizes the transactions.

Analyze where your business could provide value as a platform bringing together distinct but interdependent groups. Convene ecosystem members to design the win-win platform. Identify monetization points through fees, advertising, analytics, and services. The more participants, the more profitable the platform.

Pursue Zero Marginal Costs

Digitization allows attaining near-zero marginal costs of serving additional customers enabling exponential scaling. Products with minimal incremental delivery costs per user become fast-scaling cash machines at volume.

Audit your cost structure to identify fixed vs. variable costs. Target digitizing the latter to lower incremental costs of additional sales. Develop algorithms and automation to drive this. Outsource variable operations. Reduce marginal costs to scale exponentially.

Monetize Ecosystems

Develop revenue models monetizing your broader ecosystem through transaction fees, advertising, sponsorships and commercial partnerships related to your platform and communities. Monetizing networks expands revenue.

Itemize all major ecosystem interactions around your business involving users, partners, data, and attention. Evaluate which could be monetized through incremental transaction revenue models. Develop programs leveraging your ecosystem value. Expand avenues for exponential monetization.

Engineer Demand Velocity

Exponential profit models engineer demand velocity into marketing and sales models through viral loops, automated sales funnels, and AI-optimized conversion. Higher velocity lowers acquisition costs enabling exponential scaling.

Analyze conversion rates identifying key friction points and bottlenecks. Develop automation, viral and AI driven approaches to accelerate and optimize conversion. Lower sales costs through marketing automation. Higher velocity creates exponentially reduced acquisition costs.

Drive AI Optimization

Machine learning algorithms and AI optimization adjust pricing, optimize perfect bundles/offers, match customers to products, and maximize lifetime value. AI drives exponential profit gains.

Define optimization objectives, data pools, and algorithms to enable AI learning and profit optimization. Focus AI on highest value impacts first. Implement continuous improvement. Expand AI over time to exponentialize all profit dimensions including pricing, bundling, allocation, and churn reduction. AI optimization compounds profits.

By reengineering profit models to capture nonlinear economics, organizations sustain profitability amidst exponential growth. Traditional models restrict, while exponential models incentivize growth. Combine the above to architect your exponential money machine!

Chapter 13: Developing Exponential Leaders

Realizing exponential visions requires developing leaders who can inspire 10X thinking in others, build high-performing exponential teams, and architect exponential business models. This final chapter reveals how to cultivate exponential leaders.

John Bouter has mentored dozens of exponential leaders who spearheaded exponential growth initiatives across industries. He understands the mindsets and capabilities exponential leaders require, which differ from traditional leadership. This chapter will provide you the same exponential leadership development tools John has refined.

Let's explore the various dimensions of exponential leadership. While technical skills are trainable, exponential leaders require particular mindsets, creativity, and vision to thrive in uncertain environments. Combined, these attributes empower leaders to craft bold futures and rally others to turn visions into reality. Now let's begin developing exponential leaders.

Install an Abundance Mindset

Exponential leaders view the world through an abundance lens seeing opportunity where others see limits. Abundance mindsets widen possibility spaces enabling exponential visions.

Identify any scarcity biases that limit vision and dampen ambition. Catalog underutilized resources representing upside abundance. Conduct daily gratitude exercises to sharpen optimism. Seek examples of abundance and share them. Abundance is often a choice - teach leaders to make it.

Make 10X Thinking Routine

Exponential leaders push teams beyond linear goals into 10X visions that disrupt complacency. This exponential thinking capacity must become routine through continual usage and celebration of 10X ideas.

Define processes facilitating 10X thinking into strategic planning and team goal-setting. Require leaders pitch 10X visions. Encourage wild ideas through brainstorming sessions. Reward and promote teams achieving exponential stretch goals. Exponential thinking capacity expands with exercise.

Coach Creativity

Exponential leadership requires creativity generating breakthrough visions and exponential solutions beyond extrapolating the past. Creativity is a muscle to train.

Use techniques like design thinking, role storming, and nonlinear connections to build creative confidence. Learn from highly creative peers. Allow time for open reflection and ideation. Start small with daily creative habits and build. Unleash leader creativity to enable exponential growth.

Teach Exponential Strategy

Exponential leaders require fluency in next generation exponential business models, technologies, and growth levers to architect strategies unlocking 10X growth. Exponential skillsets demand continual development.

Provide exponential strategy education through curated readings, immersion experiences, simulations, and access to exponential advisors. Have leaders reverse-engineer exponential case studies. Ensure exponential literacy across technologies, models, and systems. Exponential strategies require exponential knowledge.

Incentivize Exponential Behaviors

Leadership behavior evolves through selectively reinforcing desired actions. Leadership cultures nurture exponential thinking and courage through celebration of 10X goals, bold risks, and visions that inspire.

Define simple behavior changes and metrics to nudge exponential leadership. Spotlight exponential role models. Openly praise 10X thinking. Allow failure without penalty if key learnings result. Promoting targeted behaviors builds exponential habits.

Facilitate Exponential Teams

Exponential leaders architect agile, empowered teams capable of exponential performance through clarity, autonomy, upskilling, and investing in the exponential potential of every individual.

Teach how to cultivate self-managed teams via training, transparency, emerging leader development, open architectures, and results-driven cultures. Coach nurturing each member's exponential impact. Guide leaders to unleash exponential team potential.

Develop Exponential Partnerships

Exponential leaders pursue game-changing partnerships combining complementary capabilities to multiply outcomes. Partnership fluency is an exponential leadership competency.

Show how to identify, structure and cultivate win-win partnerships around exponential opportunities. Have leaders co-develop partnership plans. Role model collaborative leadership styles that empower partnerships. Partnership effectiveness determines the pace of exponential growth.

Evangelize the Exponential Mission

Finally, exponential leaders evangelize missions so compelling that they galvanize exponential momentum across entire organizations and ecosystems. Exponential leaders curate and spread mission.

Coach bringing exponential visions alive through storytelling, emotion, and conviction. Guide leaders to frame missions leveraging core human motivations. Have leaders pitch exponential visions that inspire. Great exponential leaders electrify and spread purpose.

The dimensions above combine to develop leaders ready to evangelize, strategize, architect, and inspire exponential growth. With dedicated development, your organization will have the exponential leaders it needs exactly when they are required most. Now get started unlocking your exponential leadership potential!

Conclusion

Across this comprehensive exponential growth playbook, you have been equipped with the mindsets, strategies, and models required to take organizations to exponential heights. By applying the concepts covered in these chapters, you can craft and lead an exponential transformation making today's limits irrelevant and tomorrow's potential boundless.

This playbook represents the culminating work of exponential pioneer John Bouter whose career has modeled what is possible for leaders ready to become exponential. While the journey requires boldness, rigor, and persistence, John's example proves the exponential is achievable by organizations committed to realizing their full exponential potential.

Internalizing these lessons is just the starting point. Now begin applying these tools within your organizational context. Run small experiments and build momentum. Stay determined through setbacks. Keep your vision bold and inspiring. Build the plan, team and models for exponential growth. With focus and care, the impossible will become inevitable.

Exponential achievement is a journey, not a destination. But with the passion to dare greatly, the openness to see opportunity everywhere, and the relentless drive to achieve ever-bolder visions, it is a journey you can now commence. Your future is unwritten. An exponential leap is yours for the taking. Step forward with courage and resolve. The exponential future starts now!